Ladders

The GALÁPAGOS ISLANDS

M000116330

History of the Galápagos Islands

by Judy Elgin Jensen

Go back in time three or four million years. Near what is now Ecuador, South America, lava seeps through the ocean floor at a hot spot. Under the water, the oldest Galápagos Island— Española—is born.

Over time, lava continues to erupt, forming a mountain that eventually rises above the water. Slowly, Earth's undersea surface shifts and other volcanoes form over the hot spot. These mountains become taller and taller and rise above the water, to form the Galápagos Islands.

Sun and rain erode the lava surfaces of the islands; winds carry seeds and spores from what is now South America and drop them on the islands. Some land in moist places, take root, and begin to grow. Plant roots cause lava to crumble. When the plants die, they provide nutrients for the soil.

Winds blow insects and birds, even small snails, from the South American continent to the islands. Sea lions and penguins reach the islands on fast currents; small mammals and many reptiles reach the islands on tangled pieces of plants.

The few **species** that reach the Galápagos Islands have no natural predators and plenty of space. Over time, thousands of generations produce offspring. Offspring with features that help them live in the harsh conditions are able to survive and reproduce, passing their features on to the next generation. The result is a group of animals and plants like no other in the world.

Then people arrive....

Santiago

Baltra

ndina

Gabela

Santa

PUERTO VILLAMIL

Florea

1500s

According to legend, the Incas were the first to sail to the Galápagos Islands, however they left no written record. Later, Fray Tomás de Berlanga, Bishop of Panama, landed there accidentally, and is credited with discovering the islands. He was sailing from Panama to Peru when strong currents took him to the islands.

1600s

As Spanish trade routes became common, pirates used the islands as a hideout. They could easily rob ships, and their distance from the South American continent gave them protection. The island provided them with food: giant tortoises.

1700s

The islands seemed hidden for several years. Then, late in the century, whalers sailed into the Pacific and used these isolated islands as home base. One result: whales and tortoises faced devastation.

1832

Ecuador claimed the islands from Spain, and in 1833, the government gave people the right to settle on the island of Floreana. Settlers brought **invasive species**, such as pigs, cattle, and goats, which competed with the **native species** for food.

1835

Charles Darwin, a British naturalist, visited the islands. Darwin observed unique living things on the islands and compared them with living things on the South American continent. Later, Darwin would be credited with an idea called natural selection which would change the way scientists look at the world.

1860

After petroleum was discovered, people didn't need whale oil. But it was too late for many whales and tortoises. Whalers took about 100,000 to 200,000 tortoises from the islands during the 1800s. Tortoises could survive for months without food or water, so whalers stored them and ate them onboard their ships.

1900–Today

Collectors began to remove life from the Galápagos Islands in the name of science. They took more than 76,000 live and dead specimens for study. Scientists thought this was a good way to learn about the unique species found on the islands.

By 1905 a few hundred people were living on the islands. They sold resources and killed tortoises for meat and oil. In the 1940s more people came, and some stayed.

The tourist boom had also begun. In 1973, only 12,000 tourists were allowed to visit each year. Today, that number is close to 200,000.

Other factors affected the islands. For example, fishermen in the 1920s came to the islands with large nets to catch tuna. They then began using miles-long bait lines and shot sea lions that were attracted to the bait. Scientists began pushing for preservation of the Galápagos Islands, and in 1934, nearly 100 years after Darwin's

A geography born from volcanoes far out in the ocean supports life found nowhere else on Earth.

visit, Ecuador enacted the first laws to protect the islands. Scientists focused on two things: protecting unique species and removing invasive species. In 1959, the Galápagos Islands became a national park. Five years later, the Charles Darwin Research Station was established.

Then, in 1998, the waters surrounding the islands were recognized as important world heritage sites. Commercial fishing was finally banned. Today, people around the world are keeping a close eye on the Galápagos Islands. If the islands are preserved, this "living laboratory" can continue to teach us about life on the Galápagos, and life on Earth.

The Galápagos Islands sit 1,000 kilometers (about 621 miles) west of Ecuador in the Pacific Ocean.

PACIFIC OCEAN

Galápagos Islands (Ecuador)

PANAMA

VENEZUELA

COLOMBIA

Quito

ECUADOR

BRAZIL

PERU

N
W E
S

0   200   400 Miles

0   200   400 Kilometers

Check In How did the Galápagos Islands' history impact life there?

WILD
Galápagos

by Judy Elgin Jensen

Like you, I'm a student, and my assignment is to find out about unusual life on the Galápagos Islands. I can't go there, so how can I learn about them? Come with me as I do research on the Internet.

How should I start? If I type *Galápagos Islands animals* into a search engine, I get more than nine million results. Many websites are travel agencies. I don't know if their information is accurate. I would have to look at their sources.

Tourists walk right up to these marine iguanas basking in the sun.

Here's a result from National Geographic, which has its own scientists and explorers. I'll add the word *unique* to my search string. . . . Great! Now I have only 600,000 results. The first one is the World Wildlife Federation, a reliable source with experts dedicated to **conservation.** Reliable sources provide information from scientists, researchers, and other specialists on the topic. Blogs, articles written by students, and user-written sites might not be accurate.

The Galápagos Conservancy website has information about **endemic species,** which are organisms found nowhere else on Earth. The Travel section has a list of rules for visitors. The rules state that visitors must stay on the paths and have a trained guide. It seems like a "reverse zoo" where the animals roam free and the people are confined! But it makes sense. After thousands of years in isolation, many Galápagos animals don't fear humans. I want to find out more.

Each of Galápagos' islands is characterized by a slightly different set of animal species.

Galápagos Finches

When I search for unique Galápagos species, "Darwin's finches" comes up. Those finches changed scientific thinking. Almost 200 years ago, Darwin studied specimens and formed his ideas about natural selection, the idea that living things that have **traits** just right for their environment will survive and produce more offspring.

Darwin discovered several new finch **species**. A species is a group of living things that can produce offspring. He saw that the Galápagos finches were similar to other finch species he had seen in South America. One big difference was their beaks. Some species had long, probing beaks; some had massive, crushing beaks; and others had delicate beaks. Darwin realized that each species' beak helped it eat the food it survived on. Compare the beaks of a few of these species. Then read some facts I found from the Cornell Lab of Ornithology at Cornell University. Some other facts are from ARKive, a nonprofit group that collects great photographs and cites reliable references.

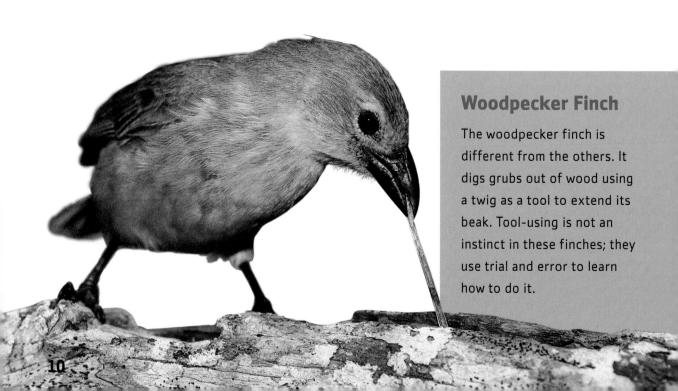

Woodpecker Finch

The woodpecker finch is different from the others. It digs grubs out of wood using a twig as a tool to extend its beak. Tool-using is not an instinct in these finches; they use trial and error to learn how to do it.

Large Ground Finch

Beak: Large beak with a deep base that gives it a lot of crushing area

Diet: Eats the largest and thickest-shelled seeds

Vegetarian Tree Finch

Beak: Small, stout beak good for manipulating soft foods

Diet: Feeds almost entirely on the soft parts of plants—buds, leaves, flowers, fruits

Warbler Finch

Beak: Thin, sharp beak good for spearing insects

Diet: Feeds almost entirely on small insects and can snag them from the air

Cactus Ground Finch

Beak: Pointy beak, good for plucking seeds off cacti

Diet: Feeds mostly on the seeds and flowers of prickly pear cactus

Giant Tortoises

Giant tortoises show how natural selection works. I'm searching for *giant tortoise* and I'm adding *adaptation* or *natural selection* to the string. Some good sources, such as the Galápagos Conservation Trust, turn up. This source says that giant tortoises used to live all over the world. Now, they live only on the Galápagos and one other island in the Indian Ocean. Why are they left only on remote islands? Perhaps there have been fewer people hunting them.

This source says that the Galápagos tortoises probably came from one pregnant female that reached the islands two to three million years ago. Back then, all tortoises had a dome-shaped shell, or carapace, and they lived on humid islands that had a lot of vegetation. Over many generations, some were swept to other Galápagos Islands. These islands were drier and had fewer plants, and the plants were farther off the ground.

A dome-backed tortoise can't reach its neck very high because its shell gets in the way. This tortoise eats plants close to the ground.

The tortoises adapted to the drier islands. How did they adapt? Like all living things, the individuals in this group of tortoises had differences. Some had longer necks. Others had shells that fit less closely to the back of the neck. Why do these **variations**, or differences, matter? The variations among tortoises meant that some could survive in the new surroundings.

Tortoises with longer necks and smaller shells that turned like a saddle could reach more food than other tortoises. These tortoises had traits, or characteristics, that made them more likely to survive and reproduce on the drier islands. The "saddleback" traits were passed along to offspring, and these traits became common on the dry islands. That is how the Galápagos came to have two main types of tortoises—domed and saddleback.

The shell of a saddleback tortoise is turned up at the neck, allowing it to reach taller vegetation.

13

Land and Marine Iguanas

On the Galápagos Conservancy and ARKive websites I discover more strange Galápagos creatures: land and marine iguanas. It seems that their ancestors floated to the Galápagos on plants long before the tortoises' ancestors. The natural selection of traits led to iguanas with different characteristics that helped them survive in different environments.

Four species of iguanas live on the islands today—three on land and one in the sea! Like all reptiles, the body temperature of both land and marine iguanas changes to match the temperature around them. They sit in sunlight to get warm, and sometimes they move slowly to conserve energy.

The sun's heat can be intense in the dry areas where land iguanas live, so they look for shade. They eat cactuses and fallen fruit, which provide them the moisture they need to survive in their dry habitat.

Land Iguanas

Longer snout allows feeding on low-growing plants, fruits, and cacti.

Blotchy yellow coloration helps it blend in with plants.

Short, sharp claws dig into soil and rocks.

Short, rounded tail

Marine Iguanas

Short, blunt nose allows feeding on algae growing on rocks.

Salt that has been sneezed out from the nostrils forms white patches.

Gray to black coloration with blotches of coppery red help it blend in with the surrounding rocks.

Flattened paddle-like tail propels the body through the water.

Strong claws grasp slippery rocks.

Marine iguanas live on rocks near the sea, where they find seaweed and salt. A lot of food is a good thing, but a lot of salt is not. All animals that feed in the ocean have adaptations that help them get rid of excess salt that would make them dry out and die. Marine iguanas sneeze the salt away!

When I look over my research, I see a central theme. The ancestors of three unusual animals—finches, giant tortoises, and iguanas—arrived on the islands millions of years ago. Each island had unique resources, and some animals had body features or behaviors that allowed them to survive and reproduce better than others. Unusual animals for an unusual land!

I want to learn more about natural selection. In a National Geographic news report, two researchers, Peter and Rosemary Grant, have been tracking finches in the Galápagos for the last 40 years. They say natural selection is still occurring. Back to the Internet!

Check In How were the living things on the Galápagos Islands affected by natural selection?

NATIONAL GEOGRAPHIC

Expedition to the Galápagos

by Dr. Tierney Thys

TIERNEY THYS is an ocean scientist, conservationist, media producer, and teacher. She wants people to understand the important role the ocean plays in our worldwide climate. She helps artists portray science and **conservation** messages in their work. On National Geographic Expeditions, she shares her enthusiasm for science with adults and children alike.

Gear up for an expedition! National Geographic Explorer Tierney Thys is introducing us to the Galápagos Islands. We'll see many **endemic species**, which are **species** found only on these islands. Our first stop? A mola, a giant fish about the size of a car turned on its side! Molas feed on ocean animals such as jellies.

Molas often lie on their side at the surface, which makes them look like sunbathers. They're sometimes called sunfish. Dr. Thys and her team attach small tracking devices called global positioning satellite (GPS) tags to molas in the Galápagos Islands and around the world. These tags help scientists locate the molas.

Dr. Thys and her team tagged five Galápagos molas. Now they want to find out whether molas stay in the Galápagos Islands or travel farther afield. While tagging the fish, the team took small tissue samples for genetic testing, which can give clues about the molas' ancestry.

Now, enjoy the scenery as we tour the islands through the words and photos of Dr. Thys.

< Dr. Thys swims face-to-face with molas. Of their strange shape, she says, "It seems a rather goofy design. Yet the more I learn about it, the more respect and admiration I have for it."

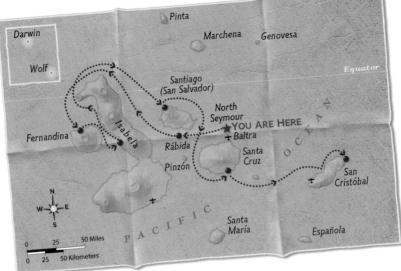

Day 1:
North Seymour Island

We boarded the ship on the island of Baltra and then headed to North Seymour Island. There, we were greeted by sunbathing sea lions. They're related to California sea lions, but they're smaller and have less blubber because the water is warmer here.

As we walked along the path, we heard whistling sounds coming from male blue-footed boobies, answered by honking sounds from the females. Boobies build their nests on the ground, so we had to walk carefully. You could call this place a real booby trap!

Bright red Sally Lightfoot crabs skitter about the seaside rocks.

A blue-footed booby displays brightly colored feet and a sharp beak. When feeding, boobies plunge-dive into the water to spear fish.

Day 2:
Rábida Island

Nearby we saw male frigate birds trying to attract females by drumming their bright red throat pouches. It takes the males 20 to 30 minutes to inflate that pouch. That's a lot of effort to impress the girls! Later, we followed the trail of a large land iguana. Its tail made the trail as it crossed the sand.

In the afternoon, we visited Rábida Island. The sand is deep red there because of the high iron-oxide content. Then we discovered a shallow lagoon, where flamingos quietly fed on the tiny brine shrimp that give them their pink color. Only about 400–500 of these birds are still in the Galápagos.

"Las Islas Encantadas are the Enchanted Islands. They are the ultimate pilgrimage site for **any person fascinated with nature.**"

The pouch of a male frigate bird inflates as big as a soccer ball! It shows a female that he has selected a site and is ready to help build a nest.

Day 3:
Fernandina Island

During the night we crossed the Equator and arrived at the youngest island in the Galápagos, Fernandina. It is a stark place, covered in lava and home to one of the most active volcanoes in the world. Since there are fresh lava flows, only a few plants dot the landscape. We landed our inflatable boats at Punta Espinoza, near some black mangroves.

In the baking sun, we tiptoed around hundreds of marine iguanas, including new hatchlings that were no larger than my hand. As I passed one, it sneezed salt right onto my sandal! We also saw three flightless cormorants drying their short wings in the sun.

Without predators on these islands, these birds don't need large wings. The cormorant's long, hooked beak, strong legs, and webbed toes give it an advantage in fishing.

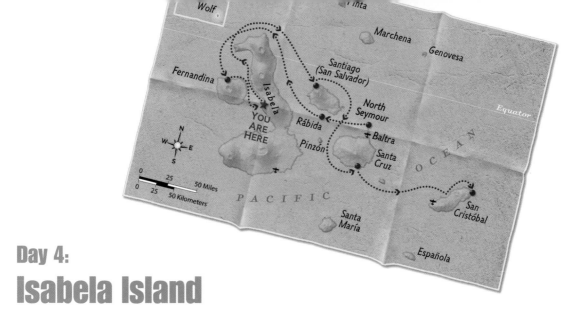

Day 4:
Isabela Island

The next day we continued to Isabela, my favorite island. Its stark, stunning landscape gives us a glimpse into what Earth must have looked like at the beginning. Volcanic slopes and craggy rocks frame fields of black lava.

We snorkeled with Galápagos penguins and dodged sea turtles bobbing up to breathe. Later, on land we walked among a group of wild giant tortoises. One even hissed when we got a bit too close.

"Under the chin of Isabela's seahorse shape, lies my study site.
There, ocean sunfish go to be cleaned by a host of other small fishes."

Behavioral adaptations help keep Galápagos penguins cool. They stand with flippers extended and pant.

Day 5:
Santiago Island

We make sure all of the guests have sunblock, plenty of water, and good walking shoes for exploring these hot islands. If we want an underwater view, we need, masks, snorkels, and fins. The weather is hot, but cold Antarctic water from the south and cool water from the ocean's depths can make these waters quite chilly.

In fact, five major ocean currents meet at the Galápagos. This helps create the incredible mix of life above and below the waves. Anchoring at Santiago, we took inflatable boats to Espumilla Beach. Then we hiked to an important sea turtle nesting site. The lush plant life here is proof that removing the goats and pigs that were brought to this island was a good idea.

"When comparing the plants and animals from island to island, one can almost see natural selection at work."

∧ With its amazing geologic features, Buccaneer's Cove was a favorite pirate haunt. It is also where Charles Darwin landed on the island in 1835.

Day 6:
Santa Cruz

Today we visited the Charles Darwin Research Station. We met some scientists there and visited the giant tortoise rearing center where each hatchling gets a tracking number.

We saw Lonesome George, the last Pinta tortoise, who sadly would die just four days after our departure. Later we walked among wild tortoises in the rain-soaked Santa Cruz highlands. There we saw the beautiful, natural Scalesia forests.

^ The Charles Darwin Research Station conducts scientific research to ensure the preservation of the Galápagos. In the tortoise-rearing pens, "tiny giants" are hatched and reared in an effort to rebuild their populations.

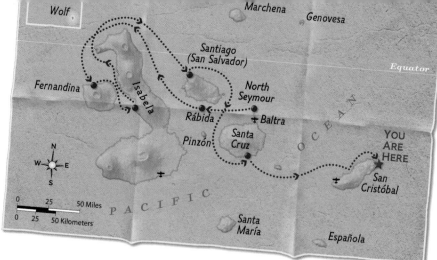

Day 7 and 8:
The Island of San Cristóbal

Today began at Punta Pitt on San Cristóbal. We hiked up a dry riverbed to an overlook covered with Sesuvium. These small, succulent plants turn bright red in the dry season. We spotted a red-footed booby nesting with her chick, and we had lava lizards as hiking companions.

Later in the day, we took the inflatable boats out for one last snorkel at Leon Dormido (sleeping lion). This rock formation is an old, isolated volcanic cone surrounded by deep water. As we snorkeled, we saw spotted eagle rays, king angelfish, and even a few sharks at a distance.

Sesuvium plants grow well in salty soil.

Lava lizards are very territorial. Males bob their heads up and down to tell each other to stay away.

The day had come for us to leave the ship. Traveling together, we all became a bit of a family. We understood the need to protect this global treasure, the Enchanted Isles, the Galápagos Islands.

We all learned so much! Even the youngest in our group—age three—could identify three different species of boobies and tell us what marine iguanas eat for breakfast. He could even identify giant tortoise poop!

"For me, visiting the Galápagos provides total immersion into the **forces and beauty of nature.**"

∧ The *Endeavor* takes tourists on expeditions all year long. Explorers like Tierney Thys travel with them, too.

∧ Even the youngest children learned to identify several species as well as their droppings!

Check In Which Galápagos island would you most like to visit? Why?

Human Footprints
in the
Galápagos

by Suzanne Sherman

∧ Over 12,000 people live on Santa Cruz Island.

The Galápagos Islands are full of unique plant and animal **species**. Unless people think carefully about how they use the islands, these unique species may disappear forever.

"Take nothing but photos, leave nothing but footprints." Great advice, but the big question remains: Just how many footprints can the Galápagos withstand? About 30,000 people live there; almost 200,000 tourists visit every year.

More tourism, more businesses, and increasing population are threats to the islands' wildlife. The islands' land and water are limited resources. Yet, most people today use these resources limitlessly.

When the number of tourists increased, so did the number of residents and businesses to support them. All these people use food, water, and fuel; they produce waste and litter. This puts a great strain on the resources of the islands.

People Affect the Wildlife

Since humans first arrived in the Galápagos in the 1500s, they have brought **invasive species** with them. Some were brought by accident, and others, like goats, were brought on purpose. Goats ravaged the landscape, leaving little food for the giant tortoises. Only 11 out of 15 types of giant tortoises still exist on the islands today. The goats' grazing also caused erosion and threatened rare plants.

Land iguanas are also at risk. Dogs and cats living in the wild attack iguanas. A pack of dogs can nearly wipe out a population of iguanas in just a few months.

Invasive pests such as wasps and parasites, and diseases such as avian malaria, have been brought to the Galápagos. Ship traffic is increasing as tourism increases. Invasive marine animals such as sea stars and barnacles may come next.

Poaching, or illegal hunting, poses threats as well. Poaching of land animals has decreased, but poachers still target marine animals. Most marine poachers hunt at night with floating fishing lines, eight kilometers (five miles) long, that drift behind a ship. The intended targets—sharks, marlins, and tuna—get hooked, along with other animals looking for a meal. Seabirds dive on the bait and get hooked as well. The huge size of the Galápagos Marine Reserve makes monitoring the site for poachers expensive and difficult.

How can these problems be solved?

Lonesome George
—One of a Kind

Solitario Jorge, or Lonesome George, was the last of his kind. A researcher discovered George in 1971 when everyone thought Pinta tortoises to be extinct. In 1972, a special corral at the Galápagos National Park became his home. His caretakers searched around the world for a Pinta female for him to mate with. Alas, none was found. Nevertheless, Lonesome George became a symbol for efforts to save wildlife around the world. George died on June 24, 2012, at the estimated age of 100.

Visitors can leave conservation ideas in this mailbox, once used by whalers.

Protecting the Galápagos

There is no single **conservation** solution for how to preserve the Galápagos, but the Galápagos' National Park Service plays a key role in the Islands' future. They establish park zones and visitor sites to limit human impact on the delicate ecosystems. Only a certain number of groups are allowed in a given place at one time. The number of ships allowed to visit the islands is regulated, too.

The Charles Darwin Research Station measures the human impact, or "footprint," in the Galápagos. They want to understand how humans affect the Galápagos. They want to provide tools to help decision makers respond to the threats to this unique place.

After it was deemed a World Heritage Site in Danger, the Galápagos Islands garnered the attention of the United Nations. Some areas of concern are: prevention and control of invasive species, control of tourism, stopping illegal fisheries, and making legal fisheries sustainable. Educating people about the importance of the environment is key. Rules for careful use of the islands must be followed. The more people who appreciate the Galápagos, the more likely its unique treasures will be preserved.

When people feel strongly about an issue, they might try to convince others of its importance. Think about how you could write about a problem in the Galápagos in a way that would capture the interest of another student. Here are some ways to organize an opinion piece about a problem that concerns you.

- Choose a conservation topic that interests you. One possibility is the control of a specific invasive species to the Galápagos Islands.

- Plan a first draft. Develop a thesis, or focused statement, that tells your opinion. Think about your audience and decide how you want to influence them. Look for information about possible solutions and make notes about the main points in your findings. Identify evidence that supports them.

- Develop your draft by building on each idea to create a clear and organized piece of writing. Include reasons that support your thesis and consider all the alternatives.

- Revise your next draft to improve its meaning and clarity. Add, delete, or combine sentences and paragraphs to make sure your opinion and reasons are clear.

- Edit your draft for grammar and spelling. You may need to read it several times to catch everything.

- Revise your final draft using feedback from your classmates and teacher. Publish your work in the school newspaper, class or school website, or present it to the class or at the local library.

> Galápagos sea lion numbers have dropped to half what they were just thirty years ago.

Check In What do you think might be the best way to protect the islands and their species?

Discuss

1. How did the information in "History of the Galápagos Islands" help you understand the other three pieces in the book?

2. Compare and contrast the beak structures of Galápagos finches. How are they similar and how are they different?

3. How do invasive species brought to the Galápagos in the 1800s continue to impact the native wildlife today?

4. Describe an animal from the book whose feeding behavior is a result of an inherited trait and one whose feeding behavior is learned.

5. What do you still wonder about the Galápagos Islands? What research could you do to find out more?